MYSTERIOUS NATURE

A CHAPTER BOOK

Melissa McDaniel

children's press®

A Division of Scholastic Inc.
New York Toronto London Auckland Sydney
Mexico City New Delhi Hong Kong
Danbury, Connecticut

ACKNOWLEDGMENTS

The author and publisher would like to thank all those who gave their time and knowledge to help with this book. In particular, special thanks go to David Klein, Professor Emeritus, Institute of Arctic Biology, University of Alaska; Julie Savidge, Department of Fishery & Wildlife Biology, Colorado State University; and Andrew Trites, Director of Marine Mammal Research Unit.

Library of Congress Cataloging-in-Publication Data

McDaniel, Melissa, 1964-
  Mysterious nature : a chapter book / by Melissa McDaniel.
    p. cm. — (True tales)
  Includes bibliographical references and index.
  ISBN 0-516-25183-X (lib. bdg.)   0-516-25453-7 (pbk.)
  1. Extinct animals—Juvenile literature. I. Title. II. Series.
  QL88.M32 2005
  591.68—dc22

                                        2005004781

1 2 3 4 5 6 7 8 9 10 R 14 13 12 11 10 09 08 07 06 05

CONTENTS

INTRODUCTION

Scientists spend their lives exploring the natural world. Through hard work and study, they come to understand nature's mysteries. They learn how plants grow and why stars explode. Every now and then, however, something happens that leaves scientists shaking their heads.

The reindeer on an island in the Bering Sea die suddenly. The birds on the island of Guam disappear. A large-beaked ground finch on one of the Galapagos Islands is never seen again. The number of sea lions on the coast of Alaska drops fast.

These mysteries were baffling. But in each case, scientists stepped in to find out what had happened. They dug deep to solve the puzzles. By doing some real detective work, they came up with the fascinating answers.

CHAPTER ONE

THE REINDEER OF ST. MATTHEW ISLAND

In 1966, Dave Klein stepped out of a boat onto St. Matthew Island. He walked around the island, and he couldn't believe what he saw. The island was covered, just covered, with the bones of dead reindeer. Thousands of reindeer skeletons were strewn about. What had happened to the reindeer of St. Matthew Island?

Dave Klein

The rocky coast of St. Matthew Island

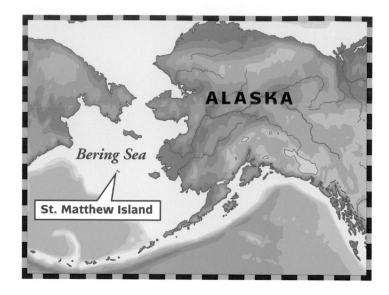

St. Matthew Island lies in the Bering Sea, which is part of the northern Pacific Ocean. The island is about 200 miles (300 kilometers) off the coast of Alaska. No trees grow on this long, thin island, but there is plenty of life. A thick carpet of **lichens** (LYE-kens) covers much of the island. In the summer, wildflowers bloom. Then the bleak land bursts into a rainbow of color.

Alaskan wildflowers and lichens

Seabirds such as puffins, murres, and fulmars nest on the island's high cliffs. Seals and sea lions fish near the shore. Small, mouse-like **voles** dig holes for their nests. Arctic foxes prey on the voles and birds and their eggs. For most of the island's history, arctic foxes were the largest animals on the island.

Then, in 1944, the U. S. Coast Guard built a station on St. Matthew Island. It was the middle of **World War II**. The Coast Guard put nineteen men on the island. The men ran equipment that helped U.S. warships and airplanes find their way across the ocean.

Fulmars

Vole

Arctic fox

The Coast Guard crew who lived on St. Matthew Island were cut off from the rest of the world. They had been plunked down in the middle of the cold ocean. What if there were a long stretch of bad weather and supply ships could not reach the island? The men might starve. To make sure the crew would not run out of food, the Coast Guard put twenty-nine reindeer on the island. If it became necessary, the men could hunt.

The reindeer **thrived** in their new home. They had plenty of lichens to eat. They had no natural enemies on the island that would try to eat them.

After World War II ended, the Coast Guard shut down the station. Everyone left the island. Now the reindeer weren't even in danger of being hunted by humans. The number of reindeer **skyrocketed**.

Dave Klein first went to St. Matthew Island in 1957. At the time, he was a scientist working for the U.S. Fish and Wildlife Service. During that visit, he counted 1,350 reindeer. They all seemed healthy and well-fed.

Dave didn't return to St. Matthew Island until 1963. By this time, there were reindeer everywhere. There were 6,000 of them in all.

However, the reindeer no longer seemed healthy. They were smaller than they had been on Dave's earlier visit. He also noticed that there were fewer young reindeer than there should have been. Reindeer that aren't healthy are less likely to have babies.

Dave next returned to St. Matthew Island in 1966. By this time, the island was **littered** with skeletons. What had happened? Dave wanted to solve the mystery.

Dave began by studying the reindeer bones. He found that there was no fat inside them where there should have been. This means the animals had not been eating. They had starved to death.

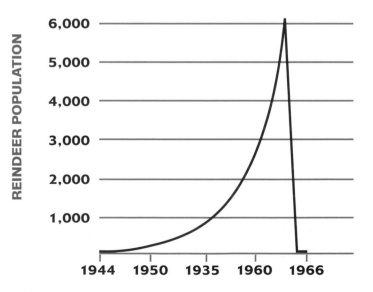

Reindeer are members of the deer family.

Dave traced the problem back to 1963. At that time, thousands of reindeer were living on St. Matthew. They all munched on the small island's lichens, grasses, and small bushes. They ate enough to survive, but they didn't get enough food to build up large stores of fat in their bodies.

Then winter came. Deep snow blanketed the ground. The reindeer could graze only in places where the wind had blown most of the snow away. The reindeer had already trampled or overgrazed these areas. The huge herd of reindeer didn't have nearly enough food. To top it off, the winter of 1963-64 was extremely cold. The reindeer were already weak from lack of food. The cold finished them off.

By 1966, just forty-two live reindeer remained on St. Matthew Island. Only one was a male, and it didn't seem healthy. The reindeer could no longer breed. In the 1980s, the last of the reindeer of St. Matthew Island died off.

The story of the reindeer on St. Matthew Island shows what can happen when a new type of animal comes to an **isolated** place. For a short time, the land that had not been grazed before supported the reindeer, and their numbers grew quickly. But the island had a limited amount of food, and the reindeer had no enemies to help control their **population**. This combination destroyed the reindeer.

Today, the arctic fox is again the largest
animal on St. Matthew Island.

CHAPTER TWO

SILENT FORESTS

Twee, twee. Bree, bree. Peter-peter-peter. Bird songs once rang through the forests on Guam, an island in the South Pacific Ocean. Guam was alive with the sounds of Mariana fruit doves, rufous flycatchers, and cardinal honeyeaters.

Then, in the 1960s, people began to notice that the birds on Guam were disappearing. By the

Julie Savidge

This forest in Guam was once home to
many different kinds of birds.

Fruit dove

Kingfisher

Honeyeater

Rail

1970s, the birds were gone from much of the southern end of the island. By the early 1980s, forests all over the island were silent. It was strange and a little frightening. Where were all the birds?

Some scientists thought that disease must be killing the birds. Others said that perhaps poisons that had been sprayed to kill insects had also killed the birds. No one knew for sure.

Enter Julie Savidge. Julie was a young scientist who had been hired to solve the mystery. Julie didn't know what was killing the birds of Guam, but she had lots of ideas.

Julie and her coworkers started by checking for disease and poison. They ran test after test. They tested the birds. They tested the dirt. They couldn't find any problem.

Then Julie decided to check out the birds' **habitats**, or the places where the birds live. Maybe roads and villages had broken up the forests too much. This could hurt the birds. Julie studied photos of Guam taken from airplanes. These photos clearly showed that there were plenty of forests. There just weren't any birds to live in them.

Julie kept digging. Maybe the birds had been hunted too much? No. How about **typhoons** (tye-FOONS)? These deadly

As this photo shows, Guam has dense areas of forest.

storms sometimes smack Guam with wind and rain. Perhaps the birds were not surviving the storms. But that didn't seem to be the problem either. Maybe the problem was a predator, an animal that hunts other animals.

Julie needed more information, and more ideas. She and her coworkers began talking to people who lived all around the island. They asked people when the birds had started to disappear near their homes. Had they noticed whether the birds were ever sick? Had they ever seen snakes near their homes? What about rats, lizards, or even cats?

Were snakes responsible for the disappearance of the birds?

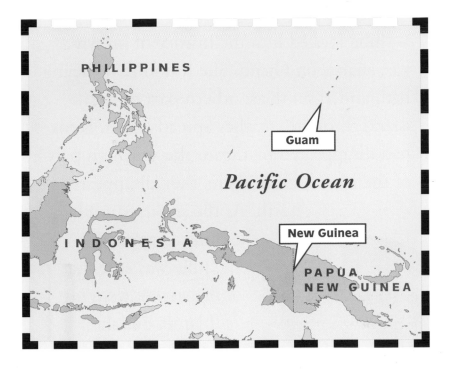

The people of Guam didn't understand why the scientists were asking about rats and other animals. It was the snakes, they all said. It was the snakes.

Julie knew that brown tree snakes ate some birds and bird eggs. But could they eat a whole island's worth of birds?

Brown tree snakes had not always lived on Guam. They were from other parts of the South Pacific. Brown tree snakes had probably first arrived on Guam on ships from the island of New Guinea in the late 1940s.

Julie looked into the history of brown tree snakes on Guam. She found that they had landed on the southern part of the island. From there, they spread north. Birds had disappeared first from the southern part of the island. From there, they disappeared north. As the snakes spread, the birds disappeared.

Julie holding a trap

Julie was sure that the snakes were to blame, but she didn't have proof. She built a trap that could catch a snake after it had eaten a bird. She put out many of these traps in different areas throughout the island. Inside each trap was a quail, a chickenlike bird. Within a week, Julie checked on the traps. In one area, a snake was in each trap. Every quail was gone.

Julie had solved the mystery of Guam's disappearing birds. Her answer shocked scientists. They had never before heard of one predator destroying an entire bird **community**. They had had no idea that snakes could do so much damage. The situation in Guam was unusual, however.

Until brown tree snakes arrived, the only snakes on Guam were as small as worms. The birds had no reason to fear snakes. No other animal on Guam hunted birds at night, so birds were not careful at night. Little birds called bridled white-eyes often slept one right next to each other. One brown tree snake could come along and pop them down like candy.

Also, brown tree snakes had no predators on Guam. Since no animals

The brown tree snake can grow to 10 feet (3 meters) long.

hunted the snakes, the number of snakes grew quickly. Today, about two million brown tree snakes live on Guam. That's about 14,000 snakes in every square mile (5,600 snakes in every square kilometer).

By the time Julie learned that snakes were the problem, it was too late for most of Guam's birds. Before the brown tree snakes came along, Guam had eighteen species of native birds. Today, seven of those species are **extinct**. They have died out entirely. Two species no longer live in the wild. They live only in zoos. The numbers of the other nine species have dropped dangerously low.

Today, people in Guam are working hard to make sure that brown tree snakes do not spread to other islands in the Pacific. They try to keep the snakes away from Guam's planes and ships. In Honolulu, Hawaii, every airplane coming in from Guam is checked for snakes. The danger is huge. If only a few snakes slipped in, Hawaii's forests could fall as silent as Guam's.

Will this Hawaiian bird also disappear one day? 25

CHAPTER THREE

A PRICKLY PUZZLE

Charles Darwin stunned the world in 1859. That year, he published a book called *On the Origin of Species*. This book describes Darwin's theory of **evolution**. In the book, Darwin explained how **species** (SPEE-sheez) change over time and become new species. Darwin's ideas about evolution made him one of the world's most famous scientists. Darwin based his theory of evolution on studies he had done twenty-five years earlier.

Charles Darwin

ON

THE ORIGIN OF SPECIES

BY MEANS OF NATURAL SELECTION,

OR THE

PRESERVATION OF FAVOURED RACES IN THE STRUGGLE
FOR LIFE.

By CHARLES DARWIN, M.A.,

FELLOW OF THE ROYAL, GEOLOGICAL, LINNÆAN, ETC., SOCIETIES;
AUTHOR OF ' JOURNAL OF RESEARCHES DURING H. M. S. BEAGLE'S VOYAGE
ROUND THE WORLD.'

LONDON:
JOHN MURRAY, ALBEMARLE STREET.
1859.

The right of Translation is reserved.

Between 1831 and 1836, Charles Darwin traveled around the world on a ship called the *Beagle*. At the time, no one had heard of Charles Darwin. He was just a young **naturalist** studying animals, plants, and rocks.

In 1835, the *Beagle* landed in the Galapagos Islands. The Galapagos Islands lie in the Pacific Ocean, about 600 miles (1,000 kilometers) off the coast of South America.

Darwin discovered that each island in the Galapagos had its own species of finch. On Floreana Island, Darwin found what he called large-beaked ground finches.

In the years after Darwin's visit, many other scientists went to the Galapagos to follow up on his studies. They went to Floreana to search for large-beaked ground finches. But no one ever found any. What happened to these birds?

Finch

Some people thought that Darwin may have identified the birds incorrectly. Maybe there never were any large-beaked ground finches on Floreana. Others thought that perhaps the species had evolved into another kind of finch. No one knew for sure.

In 1977, a young scientist named David Steadman traveled to the Galapagos to study the birds that live there. One day, he went out for a walk and saw a cave. Inside the cave, David found **fossils** of small bones. The bones had belonged to a Santa Cruz giant rice rat. This species of rat was extinct. It had been wiped out entirely.

David began exploring other caves on Floreana Island. In the caves, he found fossils of bones that belonged to many other extinct animals. Some of these animals were birds. This seemed odd to David. What were bird fossils doing in a cave?

The bird fossils that David discovered were inside owl pellets. These pellets are little balls of bone, feathers, and fur that owls spit up after eating birds and other animals. Barn owls often nested on ledges inside the caves. That

Barn owl

Owl pellets contain the bones, feathers, and fur of small animals.

explained what the bird fossils were doing in a cave. The owls had eaten the birds and then spit their bones out in the cave.

David kept studying the owl pellets. Inside one, he found fossils of a large-beaked ground finch. Now David had proof that Darwin had identified the bird correctly.

But what had happened to the large-beaked ground finches? Had the barn owls eaten so many of them that they had wiped the smaller bird out? This seemed unlikely. David wanted to solve the puzzle. He kept searching.

David discovered that goats and donkeys had been brought to Floreana Island around the time of Darwin's visit. Some of them escaped and lived in the wild. The wild goats and donkeys had to find food. This wasn't

Donkeys had not always lived on Floreana Island.

The seeds of the prickly pear cactus were a key part of the finches' diet.

easy. The island was hot and dry. Much of it was covered with cactuses. The animals often kicked over one kind of cactus called a prickly pear. Then they ate the inside. The number of prickly pear cactuses on Floreana dropped quickly.

Prickly pear cactuses have huge seeds. They have the largest seeds of any cactus in the Galapagos. The large-beaked ground finches had huge beaks. Their giant beaks were perfect for cracking open the giant seeds. In fact, the finches ate little else.

As the donkeys and goats destroyed the prickly pear, the finches' food supply disappeared. The finches could not find enough prickly pear seeds to eat. Soon, the birds disappeared entirely. Once again, bringing a new species to an island upset the island's food chain. The large-beaked ground finch paid the price for it.

Prickly pear cactuses still grow on Floreana Island, but there are no large-beaked ground finches to eat the seeds.

CHAPTER FOUR

WHERE HAVE THE SEA LIONS GONE?

A low rumble builds into a **deafening** roar. The sound floats out across the icy cold ocean. It is the sound of a Steller sea lion. Steller sea lions are huge. They can be as much as 11 feet (3.3 meters) long. Some male Steller sea lions weigh a ton. That's as much as a small car. Steller sea lions once thrived in the North Pacific Ocean. In recent years, however, their numbers

Steller sea lion

Steller sea lions swimming in the North Pacific Ocean.

have fallen quickly. In 1970, about 300,000 Steller sea lions lived along Alaska's rocky coast. Today, only about 35,000 remain.

For a long time, no one was quite sure why the Steller sea lions were disappearing. Still, a lot of people had ideas. Many thought the Alaskan fishing industry was probably to blame. Sea lions eat fish. Giant ships scoop up tons of fish. Perhaps these ships were catching so many fish that the sea lions didn't have enough food.

Andrew Trites decided to look into the mystery. Andrew is a scientist at the University of British Columbia in Vancouver, Canada.

Andrew began by studying the Alaskan fishing **industry**. What he found surprised him. He couldn't find a connection between the

Andrew Trites

**Does fishing have anything to do with the
decline of Steller sea lions?**

number of fish caught and the number of
sea lions that disappeared.

So Andrew began to look more closely.
He started looking at what kinds of fish the
sea lions eat. He learned that the types of
fish they eat has changed over the years.

Fifty years ago, the large sea lion
population ate lots of fatty fish such as
herring and sand lance. Today, sea lions eat
more low-fat fish, such as cod and pollock.

To understand what happened, Andrew
fed Steller sea lions different types of fish at
the Vancouver Aquarium. He found that sea
lions had to eat many more pollock than
herring to get enough food.

Herring make a good meal for sea lions.

Adult sea lions can eat enough pollock to stay healthy. But young sea lions have smaller stomachs and need more food to grow quickly. It's hard for young sea lions to eat enough pollock to meet their needs, even when they are surrounded by pollock. Herring and other fatty fish make the best meal for sea lions and other animals that eat fish.

In his studies, Andrew had learned that there are still a lot of fish in the North Pacific. But the amounts of different types of fish had changed over the years. Changes in ocean climate may have made pollock much more common now than herring and other types of fatty fish. A change from cold to warm water temperatures may have caused the numbers of pollock to rise and the numbers of herring to fall. Water temperature can affect the numbers of eggs that hatch and survive.

Andrew didn't find a simple answer to the mystery of the disappearing sea lions. The sea lions weren't starving to death, but they did not seem to be as strong and healthy as they had once been. Because they were eating lots of pollock instead of herring or sand lance, the sea lions were more likely to be small and weak.

These researchers are gathering information on sea lions.

Some of these weakened sea lions may have caught diseases. Pollution may have caused others to become sicker. Weakened sea lions may also have been more likely to be eaten by killer whales.

The number of Steller sea lions has dropped significantly over the years. Today, their numbers are so low that it may be hard for them to come back.

The mystery of what has happened to the Steller sea lions is **complicated**. It is more complicated than what happened to the birds of Guam, the reindeer of St. Matthew Island, or the finches of Floreana Island. There are still plenty of fish for the Steller sea lions to eat. They may just not be the ones that make for the healthiest sea lions.

Andrew Trites believes that this may simply be part of a natural change in the **ecosystem** of the North Pacific. Sea lions in Alaska suffered from this change. But many other species, including pollock, are doing just fine.

GLOSSARY

community a group of living beings that exist in the same area and interact with each other

complicated hard to understand

deafening extremely loud

ecosystem a community of living things and the surroundings in which they live

evolution the gradual change of living things over many, many years

extinct no longer existing

fossil the hardened remains of a dead animal or plant

habitat the surroundings where an animal or a plant naturally lives

industry a single branch of business in which many people work

isolated placed apart and alone

lichen (LYE-ken) mosslike plants that grow on rocks and trees

littered scattered about

naturalist a person who studies nature

population the total number of animals that live in a place

skyrocket to go up suddenly and quickly

species (SPEE-sheez) a single kind of living thing

thrive to do well and flourish

typhoon (tye-FOON) a storm with strong winds and heavy rains that occurs in the western Pacific Ocean

vole a mouselike animal

World War II a war fought by the United States, Great Britain, France, and Russia against Germany, Japan, and Italy from 1939 to 1945

FIND OUT MORE

The Reindeer of St. Matthew Island
http://www.kenai-peninsula.org/archives/000033.html
Read the full story of what happened to the reindeer.

Silent Forests
http://nationalzoo.si.edu/Animals/Birds/Facts/FactSheets/
fact-guambirds/cfm
Find out more about efforts to protect Guam's birds and get rid of the snakes.

A Prickly Puzzle
http://www.carolina.com/owls/galapagos.asp
Get more information about the disappearing finches.

Where Have the Sea Lions Gone?
http://www.pbs.org/wnet/nature/alaska
Discover more about the future of Steller sea lions in Alaska.

More Books to Read

Galapagos: Islands of Change by Lynne Born Myers, Hyperion Books for Children, 1995

Pacific Islands by Katherine Kristen, Raintree Steck-Vaughn, 1996

Reindeer by Emery Bernhard, Holiday House, 1994

Seals, Sea Lions, and Walruses by Melissa Stewart, Franklin Watts, 2001

INDEX

PHOTO CREDITS

MEET THE AUTHOR

 Melissa McDaniel has written more than twenty books for young people on subjects ranging from history to the movies. She particularly enjoys writing about science and nature. Melissa has written books about monkeys, the deep sea floor, and the life of physicist Stephen Hawking. She has also written for the American Museum of Natural History web site.

Melissa and her family live in New York City, where they see a surprising amount of nature in Central Park.